Harry Moats Drives a Truck

To Sam
Danny Kyzer

By Danny Kyzer

To Sean
Daniel Ryan

For

Cousin Tripper

This is Harry Moats. He drives a truck for an LTL,
or less-than-truckload freight company. His day starts early.

As Harry arrives at the terminal, Albert the line haul driver waves to him. Line haul drivers work at night shuttling and loading trailers. Albert has just finished his shift.

Be careful, Harry. The inbound crew is very busy, unloading the line haul trailers and rerouting the freight to city trailers. Harry will take one of these city trailers and deliver the shipments on it. Each city trailer is designated for certain towns and areas within this terminal's service.

On his way to the dispatcher's office, Harry looks at recently unloaded freight. The inbound crew staged it here for the moment. This particular shipment will be loaded on the rear of Harry's trailer.

Harry visits the office to see Bob, the morning dispatcher.

Bob coordinates the inbound crew, calls residential customers for delivery notification and sets delivery appointment times. He takes calls for pickups when customers need to ship freight. He communicates with the city drivers to let them know where their pickups are for the day. He is bringing a trailer number to Harry.

Harry enters the yard to find the trailer Bob has assigned to him.

He needs to find #7714.

Harry looks for his tractor, unit #332.

He checks the engine oil and fuel levels before starting the engine.

Next Harry couples the tractor to the trailer.

He connects the air lines for the brakes and the light cord for the lights.

He winds up the landing gear, checks the tires and rear lights.

It's time to see if the trailer is loaded for today's route.

Harry checks with Bob to see if his load is finished. Bob gives him his freight bills and Harry closes the trailer door. He is ready to go.

A freight bill is a legal document that follows the shipment from its origin to its final destination.

It lists the description, piece count and weight.

Harry reviews his bills. He sees his first delivery is for Joe's TV, 107 Main Street.

Harry drives to Main Street looking for #107.

When he arrives, he greets the customer and unloads the televisions.

The customer signs the freight bill to make the delivery complete.

The next delivery is residential. Harry needs to find house #304.

The people there have ordered a garden sculpture from an artist in a distant city.

Harry carefully takes the sculpture to them.

Smith Motors is one of Harry's regular stops. He takes a few boxes of auto parts to them every day. Many individuals, businesses, and industries depend on trucks to bring them what they need.

Harry drives to Mugoff Coffee Company. This company has a loading dock. He must back the trailer off a busy street. Impatient drivers honk at him while he expertly maneuvers the tractor trailer to the dock.

That was the easy part. Harry must find someone to unload the shipment and sign the bill. Where is the receiving office?

Mugoff has a shipment ready for pickup. Harry calls Bob and they decide it will save time to pick it up between deliveries.

The shipper loads the pallet while Harry signs the bill of lading.

Harry's last delivery is seven pallets of cereal for the Marketway Grocery Warehouse. There is a line of trucks waiting for the next available dock door. Harry calls Bob to inform him of the situation.

It looks like Harry will be here for a while, so he eats his lunch.

Once inside the warehouse, Harry must re-stack the pallets to a specified height. The pallets have to fit the warehouse shelves.

Harry has lost a lot of time here. After the delivery is complete, he calls Bob for a list of his pickups.

His first pickup is at a junkyard.

Many used auto parts are shipped by truck. Harry picks up here daily.

Harry arrives at Axle Bearing Company while the shipper is labeling pallets.

He signs the bill of lading on which the address, weight and description of the freight is found.

Harry leaves Axle Bearing, but is late for Greenfield Company. The long wait at Marketway has put him behind schedule.

The shippers at Greenfield are a little annoyed. They are accustomed to leaving at four o'clock. Harry remains cheerful, but the shippers rush him out. They get to go home, but Harry still has several hours ahead of him.

Harry continues to pick up until his trailer is full.

He then calls Fred, the outbound supervisor, who instructs him to return to the terminal. There, the outbound crew is unloading city trailers and rerouting freight to line haul trailers.

When Harry arrives at the terminal, he backs his trailer to the dock and takes the bills of lading to Sally, the billing clerk. Sally is an important figure in the proper movement of shipments.

She ensures the destination addresses are correct, checks for piece count and weight, driver signature and date. She makes travel copies of each bill of lading.

Harry unhooks his tractor and parks it.

Sometimes he is asked to help unload trailers before he goes home, meaning a late night indeed.

Harry checks in with Fred before leaving. Fred tells him to go on home. The evening crew doesn't need Harry's help tonight.

Have a good night, Harry!

On his way out, Harry chats with Albert who is arriving at work.

Albert, remember, will shuttle a line
haul trailer to a hub terminal and
work all night.

Early in the morning, he will bring new freight for delivery.

Harry is tired after a long day. It will be good to eat supper and rest.

Sleep well, Harry!

Life Cycle of an LTL Shipment

1. A Pickup and Delivery (P&D) driver in Arch City, SC picks up a shipment of TV's. He signs for the shipment on an original bill of lading (BOL). When his pickups are complete, he returns to his domicile terminal.

2. A billing clerk at the terminal generates a travel copy (TC) from the BOL.

3. The TC is used by outbound dockworkers to identify and route the shipment to the correct lane, in this case, East Hubtown, NC

4. TC's and freight travel with the Arch City line haul driver to East Hubtown.

5. Line haul drivers from terminals throughout the company and dockworkers at East Hubtown unload inbound trailers using the TC's. They load shipments onto outbound trailers assigned to lanes across the system. Thousands of shipments cross the dock here every night.

6. Line haul driver from Murrayfield takes TC's and freight from hub to his domicile terminal.

7. Inbound supervisor at Murrayfield generates delivery bills from incoming TC's. He lines up the shipments for the city trailers according to their areas within the terminal's service.

8. Using the TC's, inbound dockworkers unload the incoming line haul trailers and load the city trailers. The Arch City TV shipment is loaded onto one of these city trailers.

9. The city trailer will be used by a P&D driver to take TV's to their final destination. The customer there receives them and signs the delivery bill thus completing this shipment's cycle. When the P&D driver empties his trailer, he begins to pick up new freight in his area. The cycle begins anew…

Made in the USA
Charleston, SC
15 June 2015